Grace Rises

Meditations

Prayers

and Musings

To Denise with much love)
Juanita

by

Juanita Ryan

ISBN-13: 978-1519584113
ISBN-10: 1519584113

Printed in the United States of America

Table of Contents

Meditations

Prayers

Musings

Epilogue

Meditations

Light

Arise, shine, for your light has come,
and the glory of the Lord rises upon you.
Isaiah 60:1

Light, You know
no containment

fill all spaces
ascending, diffusing

cascading down
around us all

streaming over rock
and field

rivering through
every crack

to bore
beyond wall and door

pressing hope against
our unseeing eyes

gently waking our skin
waiting to come in

to ignite body, mind, soul
with Your gladdening life.

Blessed Poverty

When I have known a poverty of health—
robbed of ease and certainty—
into this stripped down bones of a home
rushed moments of hushed and holy wonder
at the gift of simply being able to breathe.

When I have known a poverty of answers—
despoiled for a time of self-righteousness and pride—
into this brokenhearted, humbled silence
came a Voice, a Presence,
beyond all questions or answers,
tenderly speaking love and life and hope.

When I have known a poverty of peace—
bankrupted by fear and dread—
into this child's desperate place of need
came Arms of lovingkindness
held open, inviting me
into their sheltering embrace.

When I have known a poverty of pretense—
stripped of striving, hiding, covering—
into this aching place of naked longing
Jesus came, stripped of outer garments
kneeling and revealing his own naked longing,
asking to serve me in the washing of my feet.

Blessed are those who mourn, for they will be comforted.
Matthew 5:4

I was grieving—
alone in prayer
when I sensed the Spirit
asking me to place my breaking heart
into God's hands.

With some hesitation,
I responded to this strange request.
What I saw next surprised me.
I expected that God might mend my broken heart,
or at least hold it together.

Instead, God took and held my breaking heart
and gently broke it all the way open.

I was startled. But curious.
My sense was that God
was breaking through the hardness of my defenses,
in order to break my heart all the way open.
God was breaking through the hard outer crusts
to expose the hidden softness.

I saw it then, how I was being invited,
in the midst of my grief,
to become bread in God's hands.

I was being asked to surrender myself
to being broken open—
so that the softness of my heart, now laid bare,
might be offered to others hungry for love.

Whirling

Therefore I tell you, do not worry about your life...look at the birds of the air; they do not sow or reap or store away in barns, and yet your heavenly Father feeds them. Are you not much more valuable than they?
Matthew 6:25-26

I stood at the kitchen counter,
grinding coffee to brew a fresh pot for my family—
my mind spinning with the grinder.
But my whirling thoughts produced nothing useful.
And the coffee? The coffee turned out too weak to drink.
That moment at the coffee pot was a moment of clarity for me.

As I poured out the weak coffee and started again
I was reminded that worry robs me of energy
while adding nothing of value to my life.

I realized that once again I had abandoned
the present moment and the task at hand
and visited the imaginary "Land of the Worry-filled Future."

I refilled the coffee pot with fresh water,
taking in a few easy breaths, reflecting on the truth
that my part is not to figure everything out on my own.
My part is to rest in God's care,
listening for God's whisper of guidance,
one step at a time.

I talked with God as I ground new coffee beans,
asking God to help me to notice
when I am whirling with worry
so I can breathe and simply pray:
"Thank you, God, that you will show me what to do.
Thank you for the ways you will provide."

The Wonder

I praise you because I am fearfully and wonderfully made.
Psalm 139:14

Have you ever rested for a moment
on some couch or bed
and thought about the universe
of solar systems
moving and singing and carrying on
beyond your knowing?
Not the universe outside of you.
I mean the one you carry around with you—
the one that carries you.
The suns and moons and stars
that exist inside you.
The interconnected galaxies
working together in thousands of ways—
moving, vibrating, communicating.
The lights of neurons pulsing.
The pathways crowded with cargo,
traveling hurriedly, like shooting stars.
All of it acting as one organic unit
without a thought from you.
It all goes on without you doing a thing.
Mostly without your noticing,
without your being stunned silent—
hushing all other thought or action—
to be in awe
of the wonder you are.

In returning to Me and resting you shall be saved;
in quietness and confident trust is your strength.
But you were not willing. You said, 'No, we will flee on horses...
A thousand of you will flee at the threat of one...
Therefore the Lord waits and longs to be gracious to you,
He waits on high to have compassion on you.
Isaiah 30:15-18 (AMP)

"Return,"
You call.
You invite. You plead.

> But in my unchecked mind,
> the lone rider
> has become an army of thousands.
> I armor up, ride reckless,
> heedless, self-reliant
> away.

"Return and rest,"
You call.

> But I refuse.
> I am strong. I am sure.
> I am crazed.

"Return. Rest. Receive,"
You call again.
"I long to rise up
to show you compassion,"
you sing.

> I stumble. Fall. Break. Fail.

"Return. Rest. Receive."
Still you call.
"My arms are wide open
with mercy, with help, with love.
Return."

I am the Bread of life.
John 6:48

"I am the bread of life."

You tell us this,
offering the gift
of your body, your life, your all,
broken open, held out
for us to receive.
Or reject.

You wait.

Here,
standing before us,
love broken open,
you wait.

With unending patience,
you wait.

Is there a love more vulnerable?
A gift more intimate?

I catch my breath,
and hesitate—

knowing
I, too, will break open
if I reach
to receive.

They took Jesus to the high priest, and all the chief priests,
elders and teachers of the law came together.
Mark 14:53

I stood with you at your trial today,
from the safety of my home,
removed by centuries of time.
How often I have read this scene.
How rarely I have stayed long enough
to feel the stunning terror of its truth.
This was not the court of a crazed tyrant,
or of strangers to faith.
The text spells it out.
You were taken to the high priest,
where the chief priests, teachers of the law
and the elders had assembled.
I scanned their stern faces.
I palpated their righteous anger.
My heart froze. My lungs seized.
Religious leaders with so much power.
Believing they spoke
with the voice of God.
Is there a mob more dangerous?
Self righteous enemies
of all they claim to defend.
Yet, you. You stood before them,
Prince of Peace,
unwavering, silent.
In the face of terrible power,
it was you, the Presence of
love's enduring strength, who reigned.

Early in the morning, all the chief priests and elders of the people
made their plans how to have Jesus executed. So they bound him,
led him away and handed him over to Pilate the governor.
Matthew 27:1-2

Naked flesh yielded
in love
is passion.
Protest speeches
red-raging against injustice
are passion.
Harmonies rising from the soul
to make music
are passion.

But a cold, dreary night
of interrogation and abuse
is passion?
A common criminal's
grueling execution
is passion?
A lone cry of utter abandonment
is passion?

You yielded naked flesh
completely,
took on the forces of evil
decisively,
sang the love song of the ages
tenderly,
that cold night and dark day
we now call
your passion.

Nothing Bright or Beautiful

Then they led him away to crucify him.
Matthew 27:31

There was nothing bright or beautiful
about the day the sun hid and the earth shook hard —
that terrifyingly dark day you gave your life.

There was nothing sanitized
about the weight of wood you carried
or the dust you fell into under its crush.

There was nothing theologically comprehensible
about the horrors of this criminal's execution
or the ending of your life of radical love.

There were no words of comfort or hope
that could be spoken or even conceived
when they carried your body away.

There was every reason to believe
we had all been abandoned
by our Creator on that day—

that day when God was at work,
reconciling the whole world,
drawing us all into Love's embrace.

Help me, I pray,
to enter the darkness,
kneel in the dust,
let go of explanations,
embrace the loss of words and comprehension,
trust by grace that in it all we are lovingly held—
and be with you in your suffering then
and with you in your suffering with us now.

Now Mary stood outside the tomb crying.
As she wept, she bent over to look into the tomb and saw two angels in white,
seated where Jesus' body had been. . . They asked her,
"Woman, why are you crying?"
"They have taken my Lord away," she said,
"and I don't know where they have put him."'
At this, she turned around and saw Jesus standing there,
but did not realize that it was Jesus.
He asked her, "Woman, why are you crying? Who is it you are looking for?"
Thinking he was the gardener, she said, "Sir, if you have carried him away,
tell me where you have put him and I will get him."
John 20:11-15

The men came and left.
Mary Magdalene stayed and wept.
Two angels and You, Jesus—
whom she believed to be a kindly gardener—
asked about her tears.
"I don't even have his body--
even this has been taken," she cried.
There is no comfort
when love lost was life itself.
Her love, her anguish, were one.
Breath came in spastic spurts.
Spending what seemed her last wave of air,
she wailed, "I don't know where he is!"
as if maybe You, dear empathic Gardener,
had seen her Jesus
lying in the flower bed,
as if all heaven and earth
depended
on Your whereabouts.

Prayers

"Thank you for coming."
These whispered words
rose like a tender shoot
breaking through rock-hard soil.

"Thank you for coming."
This heart cry, carried on waves
of grief over the day's news,
washed ashore to lie
like a small treasure at your feet.

"Thank you for coming."
I say like a person lost and disoriented
might say to the person who came
a great distance to rescue them.

Like a person living in some kind of hell
might say to One who came
from heaven to take their hand
and share in their suffering.

"Thank you for coming."
I say again and again
as I feel your hand in mine
and reach for the hand of another.

"Thank you for coming."

The chorus of voices
shouting condemnation in Your name
echoes, echoes, echoes,
until I am faint with horror.

    Oh, most Gracious, Most Merciful God, come.

    You who take up the cause of the oppressed,
    the orphan, the outcast, the foreigner, come.

    Come, Light of Enduring Love
    into the darkness
    of our hatred and divisions,
    our judgments and arrogance.

Bells toll sorrow songs
of loss upon loss—
for lives consumed, destroyed
in fear and dread.

    God of compassion, who enters our suffering,
    whose law is love,
    come.

    Healing, forgiving God who shepherds us,
    who carries us close to your heart,
    come.

    Prince of Peace, come into the depths of
    the screaming caverns
    echoing terror and despair
    about ourselves and you.

    Come.

Heaven kissed me awake
the day my sinning self
broke through enough to
expose truth I did not want to see,
or know, or show
about my self-serving ways.

Wrapped tight in a thick
cocoon of nice
there had been no need
—no desperate I-will-die-without-help need—
to carry me to You.

Heaven, kiss me again today, I pray,
with Your awakening, saving grace.

In the late-night dark
roaches emerge,
swarming out of corners
to scuttle across my mind.
I wake to the sinister sounds
of the vast army of them
scurrying around,
laying eggs of accusation,
leaving toxic trails of mockery.
I am overrun.

By your grace,
I remember you.
And my small prayer
for help
seems enough.

Your voice whispers warm,
rises like first rays
of dawn, brightening into
full morning light,
chasing the hordes
with their cruel attacks away.

I linger in your light,
listen deeply to the balm
of your words
speaking into my need.
I rest, quieted again
by you.

When I notice the breeze
playing the chimes,
scooping the branches of the maple
into a waltz,
awakening my skin
with the cool of its caress,
I remember you.

When I follow the
cascade of breath flowing in,
flowing out,
filling, emptying my being,
sustaining life
without thought or effort,
I receive you.

When I sit in silence,
letting the cacophony
of all voices quiet,
releasing the burden
of self concern and striving,
I rest, again,
with you.

Ancient words
devoutly sung
stung my heart today.
"Sin had left a crimson stain
you washed me white as snow."
New thoughts flung
old meanings away.

Could this image apply
to the stain on my soul
inflicted by another's sin
condemning me to wander
barren earth in shame?

How would you wash
such stains?

I long to believe
you would wash them
with your tears.
Your angry, tender tears.

Oh God, cry over me
and this out-out-damn-spot
left by another's greedy gain.

Oh, that you would wash me
with your tears—
a hot, enraged flow—
until I am free of stain,
clean again,
white as virgin snow.

Innocent.
You speak this word
to a young, frightened
part of me.
You give me
to this word,
to this wonder.
Innocent.
No condemnation
for being small,
weak, powerless.
No judgment
for needing, wanting
to be loved.
No burden of blame
for crimes
committed by others.
Innocent.
Shame carried away
by Another.
Soul-washed
in the tears
of God.
Innocent.
"Hear this deeply,"
you whisper.
"Fall into it.
Be restored
to your
innocence."

Wild Fire of God,

consume—
take into the body of Light you are
the horror
perpetrated in greed and blindness
on this one

transform
to lighter-than-air ash
the weight of confusion, fear, despair
still carried in the fibers
of this being

sweep clean
as you roar and burn away
the lies
to expose what was never lost
or harmed

blaze bright—
let shine the gold and silver treasure
you hid and held,
and will always hold,
within.

You walked with me
along sidewalks today,
under Elms, grown old and tall together,
their limbs intertwined overhead,
providing a canopy of protection
against the warm August morning.

You walked with me,
waiting while my brain spun webs,
waiting with kindness
for me to remember and relax again
under the canopy of your love
and protection, covering me always.

I am overwhelmed today
by your tender mercies, your kindness,
your extravagant gifts.
I am like a wounded, untrusting
child on Christmas morning
sitting with a stack of beautiful gifts
from Someone I love more than any other.
Like the child, I am astonished, wary.
But there you are, smiling delight
as you watch me unwrap one gift after another,
all from you hand,
all from the kindness of your heart.
Help me to breathe.
Help me to soften and cry my gratitude.
Help me to run to you and sob my thanks
so I can arrive at joy's doorstep and play.

I feel my pride
slither away to hide under some far away rock—
as if vanquished—
every time
I acknowledge my need of you and
embrace humility anew.

In this place of opening to you,
I often find myself lost in wonder
at the beauty you are, the beauty you make—
only to feel
the slithering, coiling, rising,
striking of this deadly snake, again.

Teach me in my despair
over this creature's return,
to rest all the more in your embrace.
Free me to laugh at myself
and my cunning pride
from the safety of your mercy and grace.

Barren

I am barren.
Meant to be home
to love
that brings forth life,
I am desolate.

I need you.
I need you to come
into this desert I am
with your living waters,
with your life-creating love.

Enter and fill.
May all you are
form and spill
from my mind, my heart,
my lips, my life.

Today.
Bring forth
your life in me,
I pray.

Bread of life,
we breathe you in—
become intoxicated
by the hearty sweetness
of your aroma
awakening our hunger.

The fragrance of your love
reaches and enters,
entices us to seek you,
begs us to consume you,
invites us to make you
our source of life.

Bread of life,
broken and given,
we delight in the smell
and the taste of you.
We return to you,
seeking to satisfy our hunger
over and over again.

May we daily receive you,
breathing you in,
partaking of you,
letting you nourish
and satisfy us,
allowing you to be
our strength, our delight.

Was it you
prompting me to go for a walk
when I felt blocked
by burdens I could not name?

Was it you
who wrapped me in the gentle warmth
of summer's early morning sun—
opening my heart to pray blessings over
each beloved one who came to mind?

Was it you
who lifted my eyes
to the canopy of trees—and beyond—
to the mountains rising up so nearby—
awakening awe again?

Was it you
who blew kisses in the sudden swirl
of delicious breeze,
acting like my granddaughter—
showering me with so much affection?

Was it you
who tenderly unblocked the log jam
in the river of gratitude I feel for you—
Healer, Restorer, Giver of every good gift—
freeing me to pour out tears of unending thanks?

Was it you?
So intimate, so playful, so powerfully gentle—
so near, so patient and kind?
Was it you?

Thank you.

We are all so wounded and defended
and often unaware
of all the ways we spin like tops—
trying to control,
jockeying for the best spot,
managing our image,
dressing up in judges' robes,
using words like weapons of war.

When bruised or threatened
by another's spin
I am tempted to fight, defend.
But to knowingly strike back
would make mine
the greater crime.

Help me
is all I can pray.

In your great kindness
you show me
your arms of love
open in a wide embrace—
loving us all in our fallen state,
whispering to our hearts,
"Let go of fear and be at peace,
for you are my beloved."

Draw me nearer to your heart.
Guide me
in what to do and say—
that I might honor
your forgiving ways.
Teach me to receive
and be your grace today.

When storms rake paths of death–
leaving lives uprooted and bereft,
I have no power to save.

When the sun beats hard—drying earth and air,
creating death-by-thirst for everything, everywhere,
I have no power to save.

When powers-that-be oppress
because of ethnicity and race,
terrorizing communities,
leaving people demoralized, debased,
I have no power to save.

When nations fight wars that can never be won,
creating death and destruction,
leaving millions on the run,
I have no power to save.

I have no power to save, so think to turn away,
but find myself instead, fallen, weeping on my face.
Weeping for a way, someway.

Help me listen closely to desperate, frightened hearts.
Give me the humanity to weep, to bow, to fall.
Then raise me, weeping still,
strengthen me, show me my part.

May I make amends to the earth
we've raped, pillaged, paved,
allow me to see all others
through your eyes of love and grace,
empower me to follow you—
as you heal, as you restore, as you save.

Wake us
to your dream of us—
to the lovers, grievers, healers
you dream us to be.
To the makers of beauty,
the creators of peace.

Wake us
from the stupor
of our hatred,
divisions and greed.

Wake us
to your dream of us—
seekers of justice,
lovers of mercy,
humbly walking with you.

Wake us
from fear and frenzy,
to your dream of us—
joyful servants,
embracing neighbor and stranger,
sharers of heart and home.

Lover, Griever, Healer,
Maker of Beauty and Peace,
Self-giving, All-embracing,
Merciful One,

wake us,
remake us,
into your glorious dream.

Musings

We are like children
imagining we can capture God
like sunlight in our mason jar—
screwing the lid on just right
holding our unique treasure tight
oblivious of all the sunlight
filling and spilling past our yard,
running across fields,
brightening meadow and trees,
waking sleeping cities,
dancing across vast seas.

We are like children
drawing a line in the dirt
unconcerned we are causing hurt,
sure we are in the right—
that we are the ones on God's side,
forming a tight circle
on our side of this great divide,
unaware of Jesus
over there on the other side,
working beauty in people's lives,
oblivious, it seems, of lines.

We were given
rainbows on Saturday
as we stood together
on top of the hill.

A gentle rain
danced with the setting sun
making shocking
neon strobes of colored light
rise up from our feet
and arch in double ecstasy
across the sky.

Two separate, complete rainbows
united in their celebration of hope.

"Rainbows are a promise,"
I whispered in your ear.

Their westward feet were so close
to our own
that I reached to touch them.
But they eluded me.
Our eyes witnessed
what our hands
could not hold.

Rainbows.
Promises.
Oh, God,
help us to hope.

I have been staring at that door again,
perhaps because people I know
are lining up at it,
reluctantly
taking numbers.
I cry when they pass through and
are gone from sight forever.

I've sat near the door,
from time to time, keeping
people company in their waiting—
sensing, at times, a crowd
of angels and loved ones
pressing close,
waiting with us,
while we've read a psalm, held hands
and kept trying to breathe.

I've heard the stories
about the other side.
Stories of so much love that you feel
your skin might not contain you
and your heart will surely burst.
Stories about beauty beyond telling.
About music and so much color.
Stories about belonging.
About life as we never imagined it.

The door is ancient.
So many have walked through it.
But we seem unable
to talk about it much.
We turn away, resist,
avoid—all the while
knowing it waits for us all,
this door of final surrender.

Sensuous ball
of satin white elastic
you are more than a lump-of-clay.
You are a responsive, living thing.

You stretch, yet hold yourself together
as I pull against your structure.
You yield, then spring back with counter force
as I press my weight against you.

It is as if you know this interplay
will open space to give you breath
that you might rise
to nourish life in others.

Death's shadow appeared
on the nearby hills
a few years back.
In those darkened days
I was, by some grace,
given a surprising glimpse
of the glory here with us—
rising as light from my feet,
filling the air around me
illuminating everything.

Today my feet
still caress the earth,
cling, dust-to-dust,
astonished by
this temporary housing
where I curl up,
a wild cat purring praise
near the hearth of heart,
held by the memory of
all that splendor.

Grace rises,
a full moon

moving up
and over us,

building shimmering bridges
across great ocean divides,

lighting the way
in the darkness of night,

raining radiance on us
through the arch of life.

Grace, a full moon,
rises.

Morning sun
nudges away night's sharp chill,

paints golden edges
on field grasses and distant woods,

as my four year old granddaughter
laughs music into the air,

chasing her beloved dog
across the wide meadow,

unreservedly loving this moment
with all she is,

pulling me
into this corner of heaven,

immersing me in this sweet glory
you have given us to share.

I am stumbling down, stupid drunk—
inebriated on spiked slogans
and sophisticated appeals
poured freely
from screens, billboards, magazines,
lulling me
into an intoxicated stupor
until my brain is pink cotton candy fluff,
my senses numb—
so that I can no longer clearly see or feel
the natural world
or all that matters most.
All I want is more.

You gaze down on us
like a tall man on stilts,
walkin' round,
showing off nothin'
but your golden smile—
you are a spy with hat pulled low.

What do you see,
new moon,
as you survey
this blue marble?

You, who inspire love songs,
when you bare all,
do you see us loving
this breathing beauty
we are called
to husband?

Bare your face.
Inspire us to sing love
to this sapphire lady
with our living--
protectors, caretakers,
healers, amends makers--
teach us the songs
of love.

I sit near the window in the diner,
wrap hands around a warm white mug,
and gaze back
across the boulevard to the hospital,
aware that this day's solo wait
for my love
is an early drill of things to come.

Aware that as sure as winds sweep
riotous autumn leaves from the trees,
as sure as migrating geese
wing their way out of sight,
today's wait during a routine screening
will one day be a journey into loss,
sweeping us down a final dusty road,
lifting, carrying us away,
beyond the horizon.

What if we saw
our faces, our bodies
as the canvases they are,
telling our story
over time
in their etchings and changes,
like the walls of a great canyon
shaped by the caresses of the wind,
carved by the movements of the water?

What if we cherished this story
and its record, written in our skin
embedded in the caverns of our heart?

What if we knew it to be a sacred telling,
one of a kind,
part of a bigger Story?

What if we saw the beauty
in the lines and sags
and the eyes that shine glory?

the one thing
we do not ever want to be true

the great terror
that has chased us for years

the loss
we think we cannot bear to suffer

the door
we hoped never to open

the path
we find when all others lead to dead ends

the crack in our dungeon wall
allowing in light

the gift
we relinquish our illusions to receive

the weight lifted from our chests
making room for breath

the ego-pinned-to-the-mat-for-the-moment
ushering in clear-eyed peace

the dying
so we can live

Today I said my good-byes to the trees
that guard our street and populate the nearby park.
I ought to know them by name by now,
but I guess I have been walking by them
like they were residents in a nursing home—
lined up in wheelchairs in the hall way
and gathered in the social activity room,
never hearing their stories,
never pausing to marvel
at all they have seen in their years,
never realizing how much their presence
has given me until today
when it was time to say my good-byes.

It is prayer,
her sharing and
my listening with interest
to the details
of her story—noticing her love
of the memory of the taste and feel
and look of a thing.

It is blessing,
her offering and
my attending in affection
and easy delight as I follow
the weavings and wanderings
of life through her eyes.

It is joy,
her gift of herself and
my receiving of her
in the beauty of her trust
and her growing freedom
to know herself loved.

The maple shed her golden garment
disrobing piece by piece
to stand through winter's storm
unprotected, unadorned—
a gnarled skeleton
draped in ancient, ill-fitted skin.
Her exposure
awakens an ache of awe in me.
Naked and unashamed
she stands.
Breathless, I gaze
at such beauty.

I am not so much growing
        and developing,

as being undone,
        reduced.

Unlike machines taken apart,
        or sauces cooked down,

I have the capacity
        to horde my dragon treasure
        and resist what feels like loss.

But the gentle Un-Maker
        is decades patient—
        daily persistent—

working in me
        to loosen my grip,
        lighten my load.

Elementals. Essentials.
        Let all else go.

Made Whole Again

My mind, can suddenly be abuzz
with fear and confusion
that swarm like mosquitoes
rising from dead water
to dive, careen, chase and
devour all I have come to trust
of the goodness and love I have been shown.

I hear that minds are like this—
harboring hives of insanity,
waiting to rise like a thick cloud,
blocking the light, mocking grace,
attacking vulnerability's beauty,
mercilessly seeking to devour
hope and trust and kindness.

And so I journey elsewhere,
to deep caverns within,
where my heart beats out the steady rhythm of life
and lungs sing a soft song of wonder,
as they fill and empty and fill again.

I curl up in the spaciousness
of those hidden places
that ache with longing
and rest in the strong arms of
all that is good and just and merciful.
I soak in the truth of love, bathe in light,
pray to learn love,
to be the love I have been given.

Here,
I am home.
I am part of Another
and all others.
I am made whole again.

"It's nothing."
That's what we learned first.
All the other numbers
were something.
But not zero.
Even though we could
see how this big round circle
looked like the moon or the sun
or like God's arms wrapped around us.

But then the full truth came out.
"It's a place holder," they said.
If you put it behind one of those
skinny lines called a one,
or behind one of those squiggly others,
it makes it so much bigger.
All by itself
it comes in like a hero and makes
little numbers count for a lot.
And if you bring in a quartet or
a choir of them, watch out,
it might be hard to count that high.

We knew it.
That big round emptiness
so full of potential
and promise,
so perfect in its simple beauty,
waiting to offer its
value, its full weight,
to others.
Ready to lay down next
to them, hold their hands
so together they could
shout and sing and
count for a lot.

Sorrow's tears
are not hewn from rock
with axe
like diamonds

but fall
like dew
from the heart's flower
as it opens wide.

Oh, my heart, soften—
blossom full—
let fall
your precious gems.

There is something about standing
next to death
that can clear the vision for a moment.

Each time I quiet myself and stand
near this dark unknown,
a small light seems to shine.

This time, as my heart stood in sorrowed vigil,
I was given glimpses of the sacred honor
it is to be invited to live love—here, now.

I felt the weight of beauty embedded
in every loving glance, every act of kindness,
every self-giving service for each other.

I saw the gift it is to be offered the opportunity
to learn to love family, friends, neighbor, stranger
with an open, nonjudgmental heart.

I stood, awed by the calling to this labor of love,
even though I fail and fall and pray for help
from the One whose very name is Love—

the One who is gentle, humble, intimately present,
patient, kind, joyfully self-giving,
ever respecting, merciful, forgiving Love.

I ask now, with fresh knowing, that this One
would grant me grace to learn and live this one thing—
and to know it as everything.

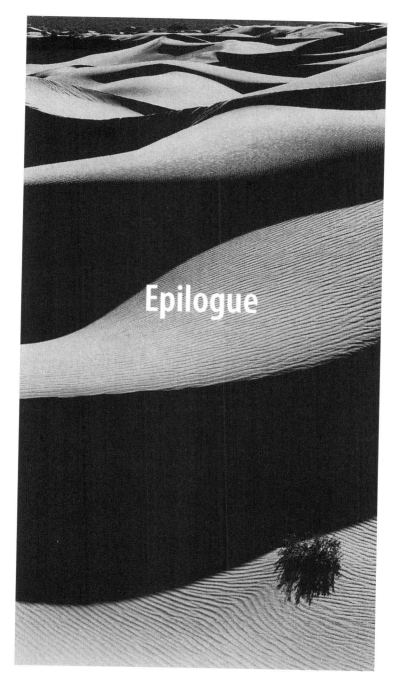

Epilogue

To Us A Child Is Born

For to us a child is born, to us a son is given...
And he will be called Wonderful Counselor, Mighty God,
Everlasting Father, Prince of Peace.
Of the greatness of his government and peace
there will be no end. Isaiah 9:6-7

I

You took on flesh and blood,
becoming outcast from the start,
forming cell division by cell division
in a young, unmarried woman's womb,
drawing oxygen and nourishment
from her teenage body.

Baptized in amniotic fluid,
you pushed through her birth canal
to cry and be in need
of milk from her breasts
and protection in her arms.

Welcomed by a kind stranger who
made room for you
where his family's beasts were kept,
you were announced by angels,
blessed by prophetess and priest,
sought by wise men and
nearby shepherds.

Sought, as well, by Herod's
men, determined to take
your newborn life,
sending your parents fleeing with you—
hunted, homeless, refugees
in the land where your ancestors
once were slaves.

On returning home,
your family quietly settled
in a poor neighborhood,
where you grew into adulthood
and became a carpenter,
laboring in obscurity
with calloused artisan hands.

II

When the time came for you
to announce your mission,
you knowingly risked your life,
boldly reminding your listeners,
(who, enraged, tried to push you off a cliff)
of their own Scripture's stories
of God's long history of including all.

You were healer, helper, servant
as you broke bread to feed the hungry,
touched and healed the disabled and the sick,
cradled children and blessed them
with your laborer's worn,
compassionate hands.

You were counselor and friend,
as you met privately with struggling
religious leaders, thieving tax collectors
and women scorned, to listen deeply,
offering back their dignity and worth,
speaking healing truth and grace
into their aching lives.

You were teacher, rabbi, priest
to commoners, prostitutes and scholars,
telling stories of a God who runs to
forgive and embrace us
when we are still a long way from home,
who seeks, like a good shepherd
when we are lost,
who sweeps to find us and uncover our
silver souls like a woman tracking down
her precious coin with a broom.

You lived surrendered to the Love of All
and taught us all to do the same.
Your love lived out in joyful service
was God's own love for us, you said.
Love that left men and women
weeping gratitude at your feet,
broken open in wonder and hope.

III

So boundless, generous, inclusive,
so powerful and tender was your love and life,
you were attacked and accused
of being heretic and devil,
becoming fugitive, plotted against,
falsely accused criminal.

Eventually arrested, beaten,
condemned, crucified,
by powers of darkness who
believed they were taking your life,
never dreaming that it was you
who was giving your life that day,

Not knowing that your public,
brutal execution,
was a gift given to fully upend
the brittle power of oppression and violence
with the enduring power of
God's self-giving love.

You gave your flesh and blood
to become love laid down,
opened up, poured out,
rescuing the world from the powers
of hate and greed and fear.

You took on our shame, carried our sorrows,
experienced the punishing impact
of our sin on others,
and of others' sins against us,
bearing even our great terror
of separation from our Maker.

You entered into all our suffering,
with the healing power of love—
seeking us in every dark corner,
restoring our silver souls
to their true value.

God was in you, we read,
reconciling the world, restoring us all,
drawing us all back
to our hearts' true Home.

IV

Your mother who stayed near
through your suffering and dying
must have longed to cradle you one last time
in her protective arms
before they carried you away
to lay you in a rich man's tomb.

For those few days, that seemed forever,
the world was dark with grief.
All hope was buried in that tomb.
Fear and hate, greed and violence,
in a world gone mad,
appeared to be the only lasting truth.

But then, God, by the same power
that sung galaxies into being,
raised you up, declaring,
"My love is far more powerful
than hate or greed or fear,
more powerful than death."
You were the Word,
living out the ancient truth,
"The love of God is steadfast, unshakable.
God's love endures forever."

Raised up, you visited many
as you always had, in ordinary moments of life.
You built a fire on the shore's edge
for your tired fishermen friends, to cook
and breakfast with them,
walked with others along the road,
appearing hundreds of times
over the course of many weeks,
teaching always the love of God for all.

"Tell everyone the good news
that they are loved by their Maker," you said.
"God is love. Live in God, live in Love.
Let Love live in you.
Live surrendered to Love.
Let Love remake you, fill you, guide you.
Be Love's flesh and blood,
laid down, poured out, given freely,
in joyful service for all others."

For others books by

Juanita Ryan

visit

www.juanitaryan.com

29909991R20039

Made in the USA
San Bernardino, CA
01 February 2016